Radicle, or When the World Lived Inside Us

HARPERONE

An Imprint of HarperCollins*Publishers*

Radicle, or When the World Lived Inside Us

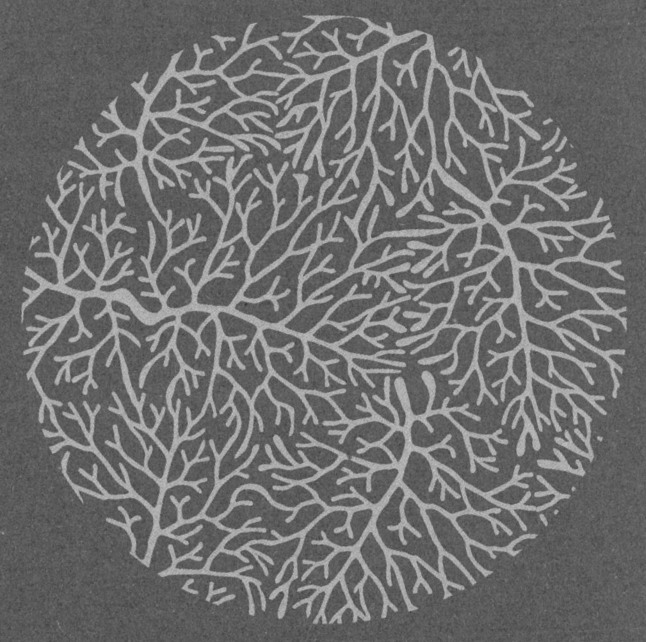

STEPH CATUDAL

POEMS

 For information, address HarperCollins Publishers, 195 Broadway, New York, NY 10007. In Europe, HarperCollins Publishers, Macken House, 39/40 Mayor Street Upper, Dublin 1, D01 C9W8, Ireland.

HarperCollins books may be purchased for educational, business, or sales promotional use. For information, please email the Special Markets Department at SPsales@harpercollins.com.

harpercollins.com

FIRST EDITION

Designed by Yvonne Chan
Tree roots illustration © naphatcha/stock.adobe.com
Paper texture background © Pădureț Dan-Cristian/stock.adobe.com
All other illustrations © Sarah Kellogg

Library of Congress Cataloging-in-Publication Data has been applied for.

ISBN 978-0-06-341455-6

25 26 27 28 29 LBC 5 4 3 2 1

Radicle:

Merriam-Webster: The root of a plant embryo.

Britannica: The first organ to appear when a seed germinates. It grows downward into the soil, anchoring the seedling.

For Poppy, Iris, and Harper

At the end of my suffering, there was a door.

—Louise Glück

Contents

Anchor

Introduction

I haven't always been the person I've wanted to be, but I'd like to think, as I approach midlife, that I'm moving closer to her. Right now, I'm watching a final few leaves cling to the aspens, the emerald glow of summer having long given way to fall, and I'm thinking of the endlessness of it all, that nothing is ever final. I remember learning about the life cycle of aspens when I first moved to northern Arizona; how new shoots sprout directly from existing roots of mature trees—an entire grove originating from a single seed.

Standing in a quaking field, I can't help but feel that aspens are a lot like womanhood—giving of themselves in weightless appendage, their phases of growth and decay carried by the seasons to establish something both ancient and new as the years extend.

There was a time in my life when I didn't see a path forward. In darkness, poetry was a tether to myself, often in reflection and marvel of nature's authenticity. Now, as I raise three daughters in a burning world, it's easy to fall back into the despair of uncertainty.

But then, I look at the aspens.

What I want to say to you in these poems is what I will tell each of my daughters as they grow: that we have inside us the root of every origin, the spark of self embedded in these strong and bounded bodies. And within that radicle lies the interminable ability to begin again, to create something vast—blooming and worn—no matter how lost we become.

—Steph Catudal

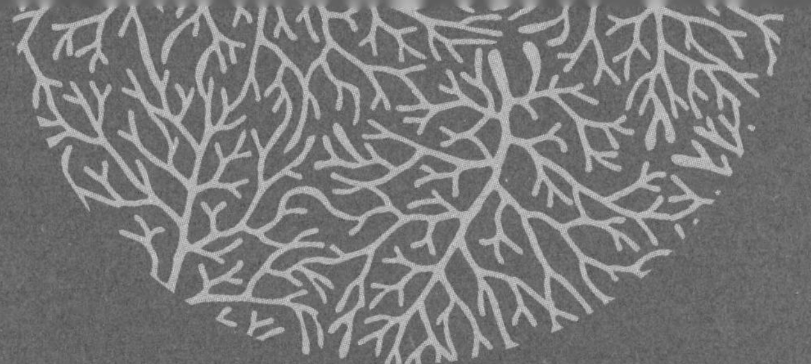

Germinate

Radicle

she was once a redwood
pithy bark towered high
crimson branch a fortress among sorel and fern
watching evolution stake claim above her roots
she adapted—
            slow deposits
under the canopy of her reach
building empires,
she tethered worlds

in a way,
my god,
                        she was god

and now, a whisper of Artemis

stripped bare she is
rebirthed, a sprout
tender and meek
carrying it all as
embryo of a new life
she can't yet see
so please
hold her gently—
fragile leaves so green, they reach and she wonders
if grief connotes this evolution

in dreams she cries *but I used to be a redwood*

as though she did not still have
inside her
all that is needed
to begin again

as though it was the trunk,
            not the seed,
         that makes a giant

On Becoming a Precious Thing

the egret struggles across bermudagrass
determined against a mighty wind,
neck plumed in question:

remember how we stumble,
how we drag ourselves
across wild plains?

while a mother
soothes her baby in the checkout line
cradling a love
of devoted exhaustion,
hands spilling with nascent wonder:

remember
how the fullness of life
was once held in our arms,
when the weight of purpose
was a cooing twenty pounds?

she comforts   &
          could I?

shelter my innocence
with the awed dedication
my mother once offered me,
hold my
infancy with a hope so raw

I'm drawn to recall
how we all
come into this world
as egret and wind,
mother and baby,
one who carries and
allows herself
to be carried

could I allow myself to be that

precious,

budding thing?

all soft and open,
full of promise,
still growing

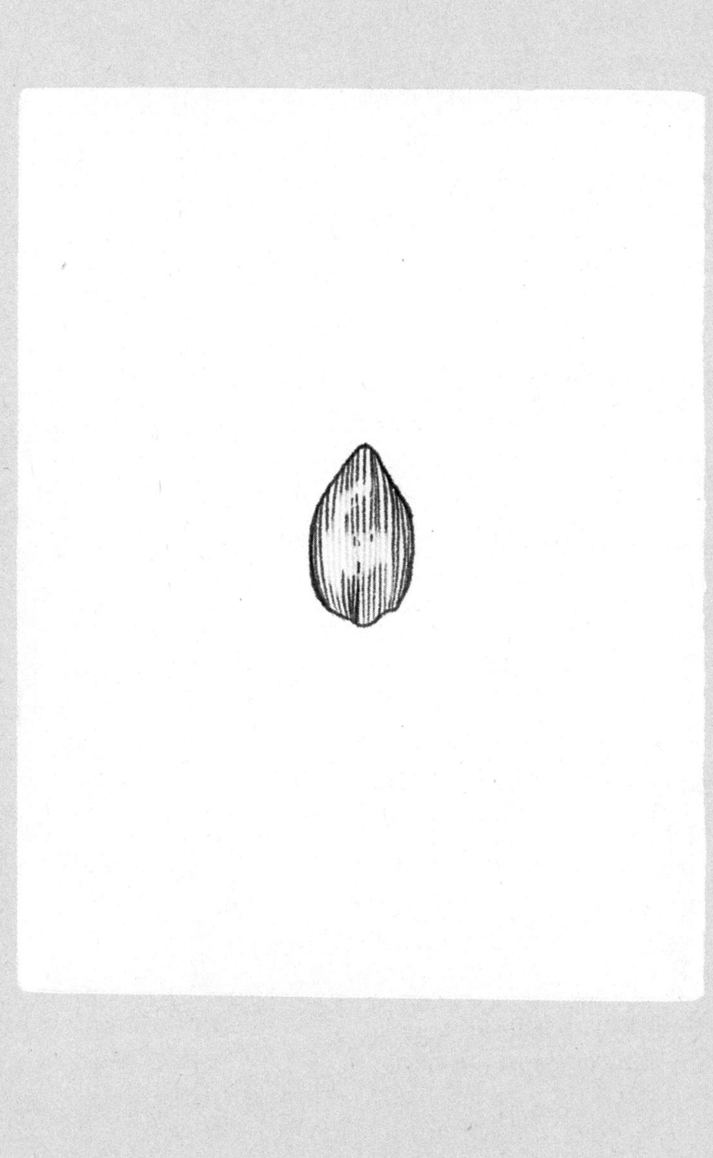

In the Bleak Midwinter

bird of prey
devours the flesh
long before we concede to dust

bones splayed for wolves
I whisper a name that is rarely called,
searching for sere silhouette
beyond the ash and haze

but when my daughter studies the fault lines of my face
and the soft edges that feel foreign to me now—
are they not what grew her, fed her, carried her?

a smile carved across this thirsty desert
every tear a riverbed—
the trenches I smooth and fill
hew the terrain of her memory

listen: she too will grow old
and the weathered landscape she curses
will tell of the things I loved most—
gorge of sorrow, fickle winds of joy
valley of every heartbreak, every triumph
mapped on her tired and aging skin

and with faltering arms
she will lay me in the earth

as something lived
something loved
something whole

and my body will give way
to grow and hold what's new again

Indentation of Life

You die in my dreams.

Not every night but
often enough to let them
take shape:
hot flashes of sunken faces,
fevered nights in
gullied skin and
hands too bony
to hold, your body
shale in my arms,
a burden so holy it feels
like worship
though your memory
haunts me
when I wake to find you,
not a living thing but some
indentation of life

(the piano bench
still holds your shape)

phantom melody
or
a reminder that love does not
abide
inside
the body?

Here we outlive impermanence.

Still my father:
an infinite refrain.

I reach for you and think
maybe death
isn't an end
at all

Pinnacle

You came out growling,
fluid and
expansive
lead by the virtue
of your own unfolding.

If anyone ever argued the autarchy
of a binary world
I would say
look, see this child:
embodiment of integration
sacrament of duality
once revered as deity
archetype of
that beautiful,
holy
gray.

How did someone so stunted
birth the whole future?

(we do, we do)

Somehow this broken body
hosted the grail of its own sage

(it does, it does)

Oh, new earth,
teach me
to be liminal—
to find myself on tender fray
and watch the world bend around me
rather than

draw a line
        parse the sides
                and call it god.

Coming Home

Winter's gray knits into spring
paris green,
tender bellied with promise
across glowing fields of brittlebush.

The fledgling our daughter nursed in October
has found its way back to the oak tree,
scattered wings now full he returns
            from the fall.

Out back my husband plants tomatoes
following May's final frost—
thumb down in loam he pushes
the beginning of every living thing.

As cerulean folds to fire
we will watch them grow,
seed to stem to flower to fruit
before submitting
to the hardening.

I have inside me all seasons,
the spark of every origin,
my long abiding revival.

Be patient while I shed this brumal skin:

a crow finds the air
    the sprout shows its roots
        this world was drawn for change.

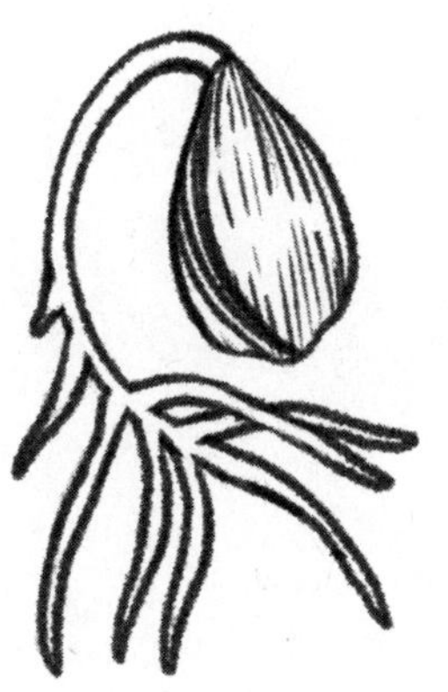

New Moon

I give you my love and
I give you this anger,
embers of an untamed inheritance.

How will it forge you?

I wrap my arms around you and
wrap you in this sorrow,
deep well I've always known.

How will you bend?

Here I am: a child
offering fragments of life,
tapestry pieced together
for you.

Is it enough to keep you warm
through this wintered adolescence?

The foal falters across the pasture,
legs shaking under new weight
while the mare leads boldly,
unable to see
beyond the range.

I speak guiding words
            with a heavy tongue—
bridle and reins in this humbled mouth.

What of my stuntedness will you carry?
What of my brokenness will break you, too?

The sky is clear tonight,
we trace constellations:
Centaurus, Crux, The Southern Cross.

I want to apologize
to this young heart
I carry
like war cry
and white flag.

Instead I offer myself,
give these wild gifts
        and say

Look!
the moon shines a crescent
from where we sit
but up there
she's always whole.

Wild Iris

This place is a cornfield,
rows of Painted Mountain
tipping towards September,
green and gold lit up like Christmas
across our autumn sky, that
arrogant in-between, that's how it feels
to leave you, can barely see my way through silk and ears
and it's almost harvest,
almost time to let you go
wherever the barreled hum of life
might take you.

Lost in the furrow
I run,
brace aging arms
around what once grew inside
but you are a field, now,
sprawling and full.

Did I tend you well?
Till the fertile soil of your unworldliness
with the love it requires to become
something in this world?

Please,
if just one thing,
let it be happy.

New Skin

It's 2am when my daughter finds our bed, quiet tears bending half-light as she curls her back against my belly in search of perfect warmth and muted noise and innocence of fear, long limbs spilling over the mattress as she finds her way to me, skin on skin, shifting closer still.

I want to pull her *up*, hold her in the forge of my body, consume her fears until they become my own, return to when her happiness lived in the firmament of my womb.

Instead I trace the curve of her spine—oh, lineage of life—the pain of growth stretched beyond whimsy, the husk of childhood shedding quickly now, though in this gloaming she still feels like something I can cradle.

How it stings to be a new thing loosed on a cruel planet. How it aches to let her discover the hurt of it, exposed to the imminent dawn.

And still she threads her body against mine, skin on fire, searching for home.

Satellite

To hold you long after you're gone
remembering when there was no mooring
but the surety of your touch,
when the sun rose and set on the arch of that mount,
Sisyphus and his rock only my burden
was love.

And now I am loosed—
                    ellipses of myself
orbiting the briar and sunworn grasses
of an empty nest
because that's how I lived—
always circling round some other thing,
not hunter and prey
but a
vulturous excuse for my
failure to land.

Who am I without you,
my gentle tomorrow?

I spent half a lifetime
navigating your world
only to find
I had been trying to shape
the universe.

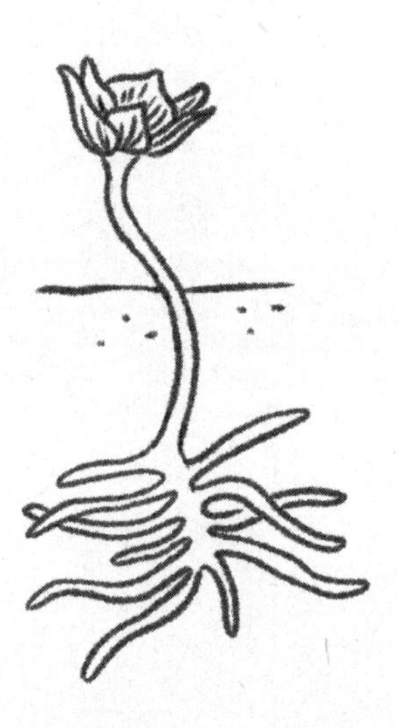

Feeling for Tumors

To be a poet you must bleed, they say
skin pinched between fingers, feeling for
tumor;
hold the pulse of humanity,
spill yourself out,
bleed it dry and the art
will come.

So I pinch, I feel, I bleed
but in that posed pressure \ skin against skin
hands searching for the ache,
I find something in addition to
pain.

There is always tumor
in this malignant world
—and yet—
between curious fingers
no matter the mass
I find love.

Sonora

The only time you saw me cry
was when he sent me flowers.

Outside the mesquite were twisted in their
spectred ways and I felt just as bent,
just as haunted—
mouth open like some
effigy of barren silence.

That's just how I am.
How else am I supposed to be
when everything around is
dead or dying?

Anyways, it's
not as uncomfortable as it seems,
I said,
the elements shaped me this way
and look:
sometimes a bird or
another living thing chooses
to love me or
makes me its home.

And you stared at me like some revenant,
like grief had killed you once
but brought you back
just in time for mine.

Dahlias in hand you
traced the name on the card
not knowing how to hold me,
my body a knotted trunk
inconsolable
in the vast desert of my sorrow.

LITTLE DEATH

To live you must first
die a little death.

My father and I talk of this sometimes,
him having died dozens of little deaths,
a blaze of atoms
as my mother waited for him in the flesh
on the other side of things.

I ask him what it was like
to die a little,
to become unbounded whisper
in this corporal world.

Fire moves across the dawning sky,
the moon a titian flicker,
refracted relic of light.

My mother sleeps,
he sips his coffee.

Warmth and particles, he says
Warmth and particles.

I imagine his hand on the mug,
take note of its weatherance,
the topography of age a relief I've come to see
as clemency.

If I believed in god I'd say grace
but instead I just
can't believe my luck.

My father who was once
warmth and particles has returned to this
aching body this tepid coffee this sleeping house his
moonlit wife
this ever-ebbing world
so fractured, so full.

I reach for the apparition, return to child.

To die a little death is
to recall that which
keeps us whole,
to gather the pieces
and choose this life
over and over.

Grow

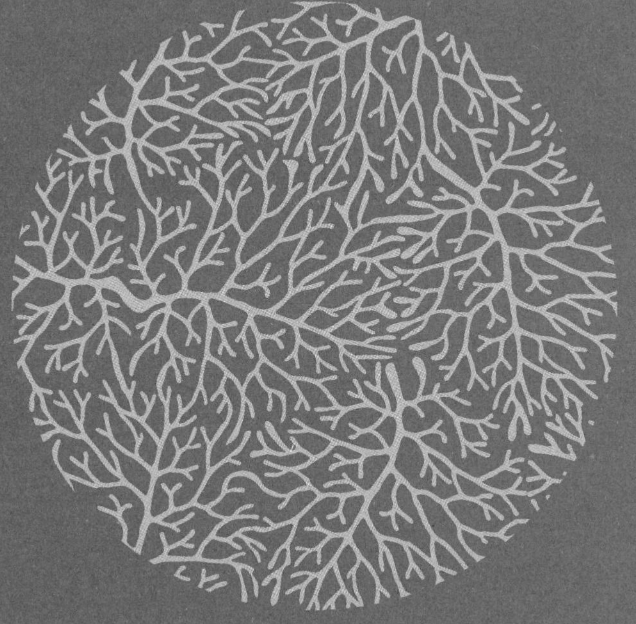

The Whispering Season

I blame myself
for the fallen leaves this year.
Desiccated, curled like claws
they reach from the rotting ground
skeletal and submitted
while under foot,
the slow end of things
comes like a rapture.

Molded layer littered with summer's splendor
I can hear its sorrowed song:
what was once so alive has fallen
chartreuse to sullen brown
weeping truths
found only
in this
whispering season.

If I'm the reason for this decay
tell me it was worth it,
that I will relent to the frost
only to return next year
in a pageant
of perennial bloom.

The Starting Line

It's easy to forget
the quaking steps that led us here.

I thought I'd always remember
how precious it is
to breathe, to walk,
to wake with eyes wide open
but here I am now, unable to recall
the sweet desperation
reckoning with impermanence
can bring.

It's easy to forget
our fragility,
how being alive is exquisite and rare.

And then she reaches for the monarch
perched on milkweed,
her small hand yearning to hold
the brittleness of life.

Beauty abounds even as the world burns.

The greatest act of rebellion
was not a battle cry—
it was a breathless whisper.

It was our daughter
reaching for beauty
despite its frailty,
unaware of how easily
things
fall
apart.

It was you, knowing these things
and still
moving forward
in small,
quaking steps.

Growth Is Its Own Kind of Grief

Small one
when did we part?

Feels like yesterday I traced
velvet skin,
tiny fingers that found my face
in the dark
stopped searching as you grew.

How you grew.

I reach
across this new distance—
in the space you once lived,
a hollow cove.

Your body no longer folds
into mine.

There is a clear line, now,
between where I end and
you begin.

It is lovely, it is tragic that we must

s e p a r a t e

for you to become,
that again I must shed
pieces of myself
for you to exist.

But then you take my hand before bed,
ask that the door be left cracked open,
to let the light in
just a bit.

Maybe this is your new way of
finding my face,
of saying
 you are
not yet ready for
the great alone.

So I leave the door open.

Even as we age
          you
find me in the dark.

No, this change isn't a loss
   but a reminder that
  our love is an empire
          built
 when the world lived inside me.

The Caregiver

It was all brawn and instinct, that's how she did it/

waking to the rising sun if not a twilight call asking
consent to open his body, fit it with a new tube new line
new chemical/ bedside table littered with scriptures and
chip bags and prescription pills there was no glamour no
piety just the lowly remnants of hopesick survival.

I once spent a summer laying sod, hauling dank rolls
of grass from the flat of an old Chevy, laying them one
by one until my arms gave out. There was symmetry in
unfurling cylinder to square/tight rows of Kentucky Blue
across lines of soft dirt as spring stretched to June, callow
world aching with new life.

She cared for him like a newborn, skin so thin she
fed him bathed him walked him carried him when he
woke at all hours, his body rejecting this departing
form/ when she loved him more than she ever thought
possible, emboldened by the impossible task of keeping
him alive.

She loved him bare boned and pallid, fetal and budding
while he planted roots in foreign land, tired hands tilling
the wild earth of his body.

When people ask how she did it I want to liken it to
something bold but all I can think of is that summer
laying sod, unwinding nascent life across fresh soil, finding
symmetry across lines of beauty and pain/

all brawn and instinct she carried the weight until her
arms gave out.

Ceasefire

The olive tree ignores her sparseness
the trunk, the branch, the terra rossa soil
can't tell where
one begins and
the other ends

            out here

what a revelation, to pay no mind to what we lack,
            to let roots grow beyond lines drawn in limestone

to live and stretch and
breathe in negatives.

By nature we defend deficiencies,
  made full by the spaces between:
the bluebird sky, the sun that nourishes
through glimpses of crown shyness

by design existence is not
determined by beginnings and ends
but through the wholeness of its cycles;

(how we feed each other)

& when a mother dies
part of her lives on
in 7 pounds of flesh,

desperate for affection and then
desperate to give it

𝄆

how is it a rebellion to ask for an end
to this killing
when
we're all just
dying to love?

The Gardener

I killed the basil while you were away
not intentionally, it was
murder by omission.

I didn't think about plants in your absence,
about small white flowers or their arching, glossy leaves
that demand the smallest kindness
to stay alive.

I'm not meticulous,
not the type of woman that
plans watering days
or
play dates or meals
or
opens the curtains before
leaving home.

And still

upon your return
you smiled
at the basil's parched stem,
pulling me in,
knowing how to tend fragile things
that wilt in the absence
of enduring light.

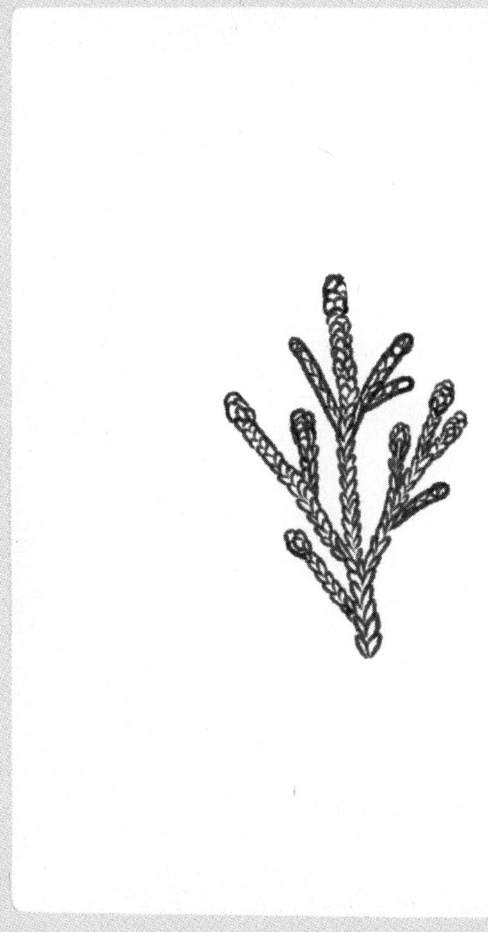

(saudade)

I miss my sadness,
how it felt in my hands,
its suppleness,
its ease.

I could offer it like an excuse,
marauding for approval:

Look, see!
there's a reason I am
the way that I am
            all
soapstone and alabaster
inside this hardened skin.

I miss the weight of it,
the blanket I reach for—
a soft comfort to bury me.

I'm exposed in this light,
hot morning of joy
anchored in the marrow.

I sip my coffee, draw my daughters in.

There is a brown bear
grazing out back
drunk on young shoots offered

in this timid spring,
azure sky so tame.

Does she long for winter,
when the grasses are withered and spent?

For the season that whispers
in its starkness

a reason to be still.

Screaming Saucers

It is strange the things we remember, you said
like how you recall finding
a garter snake in the cupboard
when you were looking for an onion
but not
what color shirt he wore
when you brought him home
from the hospital.

It's funny, you said. I remember the silliest things:

the robin perched on poplar
the smell of late October in Montreal
the potted hibiscus' final bloom
the sour penny candy from
Montrose depanneur—
how it left a blue film
on our fingers,
how you despised it but
let us eat it anyways.

Screaming Saucers!
you yelled from the kitchen
I remember the name I remember the smell
I remember these things
but not
his last meal or
how he looked when he cried or

what it sounded like
when he drew
his last breath.

I wonder, you said. I wonder if the mind forgets
the things too heavy to carry
around in our bodies.

I nodded, my belly ripe with life,
the powdered blue on my fingers
a childhood memory.

But
I remember
I remember
I remember the color, the look, the sound,
how it stuck to my fingers,
how it sticks to my bones.

I remember it all

Is that
why I feel
so heavy?

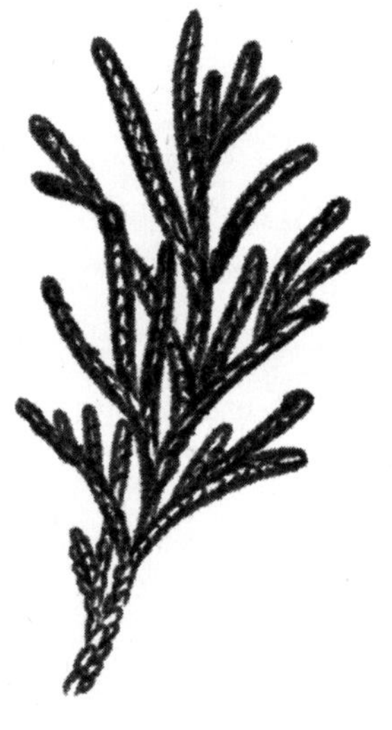

Christmas Eve

after "Field Bling" by Ada Limón

It's been a long time since I've wanted to die.
You almost forget how it feels.
The sunset is gorgeous tonight,
misted gold across a seasoned sky, the swell so high
the lifeguards have cordoned off the beach.
Maybe later I'll walk past the yellow tape,
dip my toes in the water
to remind myself how it feels to be
on the edge of things
when everything else
burns beautiful.
Then I'll turn around,
walk home to my daughters
curled up in Christmas pajamas
and say
I can't wait for tomorrow.

Some Things Are Not Meant to Be Fixed

Between the poplars was a treehouse—
plywood and strand board nailed to
slender limbs that reached
beyond the lilac,
leaves rustling like maracas in July,
barren branches haunting come October.

It was Easter when I fell
through a hole
in the floorboard,
moist ryegrass under my back
before my father
gathered me up,
violet tulle spilling over knightly arms
as he assessed the damage.

I was only winded
but he never forgave himself
for allowing a fractured thing
to go unmended.

When summer gave way to fall
the leaves withered alongside him—
his malignant body bedridden
before he could
fix anything
at all.

Decades later
I still recall
how it felt to be in his arms,
strong for the last time,
a surrendered homage to
the worth of
cracked and broken things,
my shattered heart
still grateful
for the fall.

On the Nature of Existence

For a time I was infinitesimal.

For time we are multitudes.

I was, we are.

Adirondacks

I come back to this place
honeysuckle and deer fly carried on
sweet northern air
where
 I find myself
still searching
                              for him
in the hull of these mountains,
belly of my childhood
               held in this water, this
haircap moss counting my loss
a soft invitation to
rest here a while, between
flayed birch and trout lily I count the ways
he loved me,
wondering how time ceases and
continues on
all at once,
like how these woods
remain unchanged—same lichen
etched on hawkeye granite, same
eastern pine corralling our lot
when
here I stand
a foreign woman rooted
in familiar land

Anchor

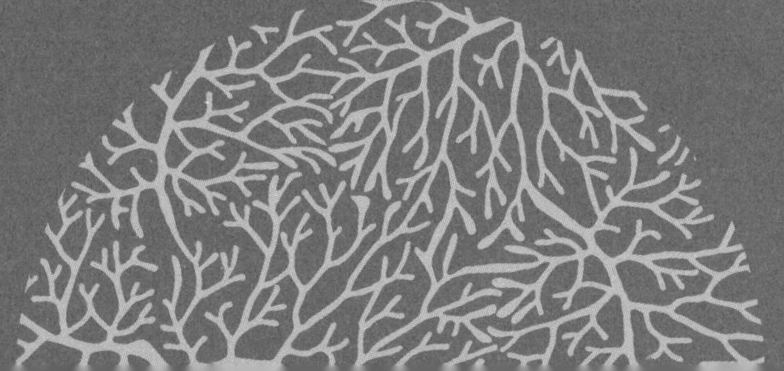

nativitas aeterna

you were
an allowance of breath
lips mouthing words undecipherable
a cry caught in utero
crusader to land ephemeral
neither here nor there
carried on a palanquin between worlds
bartering with each side
before choosing where to rest
while I screamed in deep pushes
how could agony and magnificence
edge a line so fine?

nascent skin an ivory curse
with every turn you cry for blood
more air, more air I'm trapped down here
curled in my mother's womb
she was too young too young it's all so clear
it's all right here you point in broad strokes
it's alright here you submit to warmth
and I
swaddle your hand
because I don't understand
the movement it requires
to begin as something new.

I never knew
        watching the end of a life
would feel so much
        like giving birth.

Fingers Wide

There is an old man
with his arm out a car window
feeling the rain,
fingers stretched wide.

I pause to look and there it is:
the woman stopped for autumn leaves, a girl biking with her father, a man walking his dog, the couple hand in hand.

How fleeting it is.

Because
fathers will be buried by their daughters and trees will lose their leaves and we'll put our dogs down in sterile offices and we'll all stop living or loving, whichever comes first.

And still we love,
despite the pointed knowledge of our finitude.

And still an old man
feels rain for the last time
as though it was his first:
reverent, longing,
commiserating with
life and loss
as lovers entwined,
the pain waiting behind the beauty

and the beauty waiting
—always—
behind the pain.

How they reach across the great divide,

wide.

How they need each other.

How the acceptance of our boundedness is a call to action:

hand out,
fingers stretched.

The Cost

Planet of canonized vengeance
house of opportunistic carnivore
dialectic of angry winds and exclusive providence,
selective privilege and abiding mercenary.

In the tired forest
a mother devours her young
in the high school
bullets rip through a classroom
across the globe a missile
finds a hospital
a child begs for food
a man
burns.

What of this hungry world denotes
a benevolent god?

The way you call my name,
hands gripped on hips
though we know
we'll pay love's tariff in proportioned amounts.

Stewards of a bitter world
in almighty cries
we declare ourselves
gods of the universe we create
within this holy skin.

Hollow Bones

Watch the hen gather her chicks,
wings stretched auburn and tawny,
scarlet when the sun peeks through gardenia.

Over the asphalt she
counts each one
offering cover
under hollow bones.

There is desperation in her extension,
a sorrow I recognize:
how to keep them safe, sheltered
in this wicked world.

Love births the audacity
to claim survival,
the instinct to protect greater than
her will to live.

I watch the hen and
think of the mother and
the mattress she
pulls over her children
as the mortar crumbles,
futile against phosphorescent rain.

What does it mean to be a mother
when holding a whole child
feels rare?

Samson and Delilah

My hands move like they are
conducting an orchestra
I can see every vein, see the
symphony of poison
carried through this
gossamer night—

to kill or be killed, she says
my head on her lap,
ghost in my blood,
lulled into delirium
I pull her in—
raw fingers on my chest
dry heaving
cold sweat
offerings from my other lover
as we fail to sleep
and I swear she's singing
a Philistine dream of
liquid-thin promise

she gives me what others can't
so I
lead her on because what choice do I have
when a broken heart must metamorphose from
soldier to slave in hooked iteration

kill or be killed: her silent refrain

oh but
aren't we all

seduced by the harmony between
 victim and redemption
beguiled by the assurance of change
bed by the allure of systemic salvation
                                or
the chance to be set free?

I am, I am
this is why I let her
scour me from the inside
while I
cry like a baby
searching for her father

my knight without armor

exposed

skin to skin I let her sing
tonight
she is my savior

 & when she calls for me in breathlessness
                I
call her Delilah under my breath
wondering
who would I be if

cancer hadn't eaten
my family

& when sun peaks through white linen
I
collect fallen hair
before vowing to push pillars,
bringing this whole place down
as if there was someone
to blame

Grief Is a Stronghold

you are the fortress I breach
with quivered hands
marble crumbling
as the years extend

remember that afternoon upstate?
white-capped sunset lazing over hazed echo,
noseeum & scent of trillium
gliding through as you tossed me in the lake.

"*trust me, you'll come back up*" you said
and I did—came back up and climbed to you,
over loon call and fallen birch and catalog of evenings
I still
climb to you—

past
the walls
the battlements
the keep

the bastion built from debris
of memory whispered through
brick and mortar

past my primal defense to stay submerged

what a lonely terror!
to be a ghost that haunts
only when I allow it

so
I plant iris and poppy atop the ash
to remind myself
something beautiful
still lives inside these ruins

Rebirth

We come into this world in breaking waters—
crashed against cliff
refined by basalt
along an aching shoreline,
making our way toward some stable thing, some
notion of land as though self was found
on firm ground.

And when land broke us back
we became the sea—
a wild and shifting torrent,
raging in swells before submitting
to the suppleness
of change.

In pieces
we learned
to build and break, crest and fall—
to move in lucid blues and say

take me.

The sea she gives
in weightless appendage.

Pulling us out,
we come back in tides.

Hiraeth

Sometimes when I'm out
I never want to come home

(no mom out here just Steph or silence)

I could be either but I've never been both,
never could find
motherhood and myself
all at once

So I learned to make a compromise
of marital proportions,
wed to the idea of me
veiled by my own expectation
subservient to the existence of wholeness,

a fraction
of
self at
all times

We divide ourselves we conquer ourselves take roles take shifts take names
never in full realization of what it means to be mother or what it means to be

my self

only to feel
nostalgia for the echo of lost places,
to lament a union that never was.

Is it compartmentalization or acceptance maybe
I'm not meant to be everything maybe
fullness is found in reprieve maybe
I'm never both but always
one maybe we live a nebulous dialectic where
self is found in the cycle not
some clear linear path maybe
you're not failing this earth but understanding what it
means to be water
porous and shifting maybe it's not
weakness but awakening to curl yourself around
whatever bend you find yourself living
to say here I am now not
divided but whole
in this moment
whole in this moment in the name I am called

Sunset at Freddy's

I write eulogies in my head,
sweet moments crimsoned
with an ending.

She ate pickles in the shower or
he quoted Mary Poppins with a perfect English accent or
oh, how he loved his trees.

I sift through dog-eared pages
from the pulpit of my mind
knowing regret comes like a reckoning
            when
fathers turn to ghosts,
lovers to bedsheets—
each syllable a tether
to the alchemy of grief,
where I learned to search for you
            in humble places:

the pause between triumphs,
the staccatoed touch of youth
the way your hand slid towards mine
like lock and key.

This is why I write fractions of your end—

to remind myself, always,
where to look for the things we miss.

It's Beautiful, It Hurts

I am softening to this world,
to blushing skies and alpenglow,
winnowing my bark
down to something pithy, something
new
like my father,
once an ironwood,
weeping over a photograph
of his late mother
in the final days of his life
while I stood in the doorway
understanding his trembling back
as some kind of strength
but still
too young to know
how to comfort a giant
stripped bare
by the end
of things.

Flat Earth

Beginnings and ends,
I think of them often—
how they reach for each other,
how swell becomes shoreline,
how autumn's fallen leaves
ready the nascent bed
of Spring
&
when she was born wasn't it the end of
 something else—
small fists clenched in search
of soft belly or maybe
the divine
&
when he drew his last breath
was it not a cliff
but the horizon, no
deadened freefall but

a quiet

and

gentle
            meeting?

Bright Angel

I take Bright Angel down the
south rim of the Grand Canyon
as first light
bleeds gilded into the fault.

Pinyon pines and Ponderosas line the trailhead,
juniper stretches its scabrous arms
towards
the bedrock's
staggering striations
as if the gods split the earth just so we could fathom
our fleeting hold on it.

Life withers in the descent,
green turns to ash and scarlet,
limestone and silt
sidling the edge of existence.

If life was measured in distance
my father lived until Havasupai gardens,
            midlife or
about halfway to the Colorado
where,
after countless switchbacks of barrenness,
a Cottonwood appears, then two
then three until you see
a spring
feeding the thirsty desert.

Atop sandstone and schist,
blooms of lupine and paintbrush
spill from clay soil
so abundant, so alive
it almost makes you believe
in heaven.

Sometimes
between the rim and the river
I like to pretend
my father never died.

That before the end,
before the crossing that splits this life in two
he claimed his time across basalt
and found an oasis.

The Well

after "The Empty Glass" by Louise Glück

I wanted to change, to
rid this body of fire
only to find myself
at the bottom of a well.

Soaked and stunned I looked up
to see my own hand
splayed like a root
twining down,
cinder still burning.

I reached for what grew
whispering foreign words,
pulling myself
back up
to what I'd always been.

And it was liberation, not defeat
to realize that I was not
shadows cast on cave walls but a
whole self, knowing no better life
than the one I had created
from joy and pain,
love and heartbreak
and yes,
this terrible, hallowed rage.

Loving myself has been like
watching starlings nest:
braving the elements for a chance
to witness some part of me live on,
gathering twigs and twine for
the promise of future, to
reach for my own hand,
fire and all,
and say

good girl, good girl
it's time to come home.

4/8/2024

In totality
of brief and startled darkness
dawns a lasting light

Glen Canyon

in this copper womb, a velarium
of stars yawns overhead
lucid or maybe
jaded they laugh
their
brilliance taunting my muted glow, the
way I sit
muddied in wait for things to come,
halo of memory a distended mirage
belly full of lament, they say
I've complicated the only requirement
of this brief and precious life:
to be a stud of light
against the imminent darkness
& I lie stunted in this canyon
afraid to lose
because grief is sly
love its consonance
I end things
for fear of
the end of things
but not tonight, not
under this canopy that glows
before and now
and always
a lumen
beyond the tarred unknown

Revenant

this parched mountain town
with its tortured juniper and
lupine fields exposed like foreshore
across the final frontier of my innocence
both inside and without, the way
death can go on living
and outlast us all—
the same can be said of regret and love,
how this city was all at once
too big and too small for my decisions
like a life vest coming up over my shoulders.
Was it salvation or damnation?
the line was so vague
before I sipped from that bitter cup
only to find
the kingdom I had been searching for

was me.

Peacebuilder

how do I tell my daughter
there's peace to be found when
her body is
the battleground

Kintsugi

Ten miles outside of Magome
we got stuck in a lightning storm.
Huddled under a canopy of larch
I said the bolts look like
gold,
hungry to fill the cracks
of a broken sky. To be honest
we've always known
the world was insatiable—
demanding loss in equal parts
to the devotion it's given
and we found
comfort in the balance—
that something calamitous
could also
make life beautiful.
Dripping wet
we made it to Tsumago,
bought steamed buns from an
old man on the side of the road
with the loose yen in
your pocket.
And maybe it's because
old men always make me cry
that I needed a tether, a reason to
look at you and say

that
for all the suffering
we've had to pay,
somewhere
something good
burned through its wake.

Epilogue

On the other side of things,
with its granite floors and open windows,
downslope winds
blowing off the peaks
like April,
damp soil ready for seed.

The world
once a fist
opens to a palm.

Come out, come out.
The war is over.

Acknowledgments

Thank you to my incredible agent, Tom, who has been with me since the very beginning of my writing journey. Thanks to Chantal, who believed in my work before I believed in it myself, and to Nina for picking up where she left off and never looking back. Thank you to Sarah for bringing my esoteric design dreams to life, and to Daphney and Laina for giving my artistic voice a chance in this big, wild book world.

And of course, thank you to my three beautiful daughters, who have given me the greatest inspiration a writer could wish for: unconditional love. And to Rivs, for being my love, my rock, always.